How to Meditate For Beginners

A Practical Guide to Start Meditating in 2 Weeks

© **Copyright 2019 - All rights reserved.**

The content contained within this book may not be reproduced, duplicated or transmitted without direct written permission from the author or the publisher.

Under no circumstances will any blame or legal responsibility be held against the publisher, or author, for any damages, reparation, or monetary loss due to the information contained within this book. Either directly or indirectly.

Legal Notice:

This book is copyright protected. This book is only for personal use. You cannot amend, distribute, sell, use, quote or paraphrase any part, or the content within this book, without the consent of the author or publisher.

Disclaimer Notice:

Please note the information contained within this document is for educational and entertainment purposes only. All effort has been executed to present accurate, up to date, and reliable, complete information. No warranties of any kind are declared or implied. Readers acknowledge that the author is not engaging in the rendering of legal, financial, medical or professional advice. The content within this book has been derived from various sources. Please consult a licensed professional before attempting any techniques outlined in this book.

By reading this document, the reader agrees that under no circumstances is the author responsible for any losses, direct or indirect, which are incurred as a result of the use of information contained within this document, including, but not limited to, — errors, omissions, or inaccuracies.

Table of Contents

Table of Contents 4

Introduction...7

Chapter 1: Basics of Meditation 8

What is Meditation?... 8

Origin and History of Meditation 8

Types of Meditation 11
    1. Mindfulness Meditation 12
    2. Spiritual Meditation 17
    3. Focused meditation 20
    4. Visualization Meditation.................................. 23

Chapter 2: Meditation and its Influence on the Mind...27

Conscious Mind 29

Unconscious Mind 29

The Subconscious Mind 30
    Law of Attraction... 33
    Meditation and the Law of Attraction................... 35

What Meditation is Not 38
    1. Thinking..38
    2. Daydreaming 40
    3. Chanting Affirmations....................................... 41
    4. Praying..42

Benefits of Meditation..43
    1. Promotion of Emotional Health 44
    2. Increased Self-Awareness 45
    3. Helps Improve your Attention Span 47
    4. Helps in the Control of Anxiety.........................48

5. Helps in Improving Memory 49
6. Helps in Generating Kindness 50
7. Helps in the Fighting of Addictions 51
8. Helps Improve Sleep 52

Chapter 3: Step-by-Step Guide to Meditation 53

What You Need Before Meditating 53

1. An Identified Personal Space 53

2. A Timer 55

Key Pointers to Keep in Mind During Meditation 56

How to Meditate Like a Pro 59

Day 1: Metta Meditation 59
Day 2: The Body Scan Meditation 63
Day 3: Breathing Exercises 64
Day 4: Self-Compassion Meditation 66
Day 5: Gratitude Meditation 68
Days 6 and 7: Resting and Silent Meditation 69
Day 8: Guided Meditation 70
Day 9: Retrospective Meditation 71
Day 10: Visualization Meditation 72
Day 11: Meditating About the People You Love 73
Day 12: Manifestation Meditation 74
Day 13 and 14 77

Best Time to Meditate 77

Building an Altar 78

Chapter 4: Laws and Approaches to Meditation 80

1. Pure Potentiality 80

2. Giving and Receiving 81

3. Law of Karma 82

4. Law of the Least Effort 83
5. Intention and Desire 83
6. Law of Detachment 84
7. Dharma Law..85
Troubleshooting Some Problems While Meditating 86
Key Takeaways.. 91
References... 95

Introduction

Whenever you come across the term **"meditation,"** I am certain you can already visualize a person sitting still in a silent environment, seemingly lost in a world of his own. This person has their eyes closed, calmly breathing almost as if he is one with the environment, and their face has only an expression of peace and tranquility. Right?

Well, you're not wrong. However, it is important to decode the term meditation and what it actually means for easier understanding and reference.

It is important to recognize that the ideologies of different people regarding the concept of meditation are very different. While some people view the act as seemingly difficult and boring, some are convinced that it is interesting, productive, and highly powerful. While a person's beliefs are their own, it is important to demystify the meditation process from the onset as one of the practices that will drastically change your life for the better.

This book is divided into two parts. The first part will introduce the topic of meditation and give you all the vital details you need to know about the meditation process. The second part is purely practical, offering a step-by-step guide that will make you a meditation expert in less than two weeks.

Chapter 1: Basics of Meditation

What is Meditation?

Meditation is a process where the practitioner deliberately focuses on increasing their awareness of everything that surrounds them. Whenever you hear that a person is meditating, you can be sure that they have consciously chosen to let go of any mental blockages that may have been upon them, as well as rapid thoughts. When you meditate, you consciously take control of your mind, slow things down, and choose what to concentrate on and what to let go of. For that reason, meditation is similar to training, whereby, in this case, you are teaching the brain to concentrate.

To really get in touch with the meditation process, we must consider its origin and the sole purpose for which it was created in the first place.

Origin and History of Meditation

The term meditation comes from the term "*meditatum*," a Latin word whose meaning is "to ponder." Meditation experts affirm that although the real dates as to when meditation began are unknown, it was well before modern civilization. The earliest records of the practice date back to 1500 BCE, where pictorial evidence of the practice was found, and it consisted of a man seemingly guiding a younger one into meditation, also known as Yogi's meditation. A replica of the image is as illustrated in the figure below:

Figure 1: Illustration of meditation in 1500 BCE[1]

---

[1] MeditationTeam. (2019). Where Does Meditation Come From? Meditation History & Origins. Retrieved 31 July 2019, from https://mindworks.org/blog/history-origins-of-meditation/

From the pictures, experts believe the practice was passed down orally from one generation to the other. You must note that the onset of paper in 1500 BCE is just an illustration that, in as much as that is the earliest physical evidence, the practice was undoubtedly in existence from as far as 3000 to 5000 BCE. Currently, the Yogi's meditation still thrives and has been modified and modernized to adapt to millennials and the religious beliefs of the same.

Worth noting is that the practice was not only prevalent amongst the Hindus. In as much as they have the earliest recorded history, the practice of meditation was widespread amongst the different religions and groups of people around the world. That notwithstanding, many scholars are inclined toward the belief that meditation stemmed from the Hindus, and any adaptations done by other groups were a result of influence from said Indian people.

Some of the notable groups who embraced meditation early on include:

- Buddhists
- Greeks
- Shamans
- Wiccan religious people

- Christian Mysticisms
- Sufists in Islam
- Jews

All the groups mentioned are known to have adopted meditation many centuries ago for different reasons. While the practices and ideas behind their meditations are different, the fact remains that it is the same practice. All meditation encompasses awareness and concentration, and all must be done in a serene and silent environment. Also, the outcome of the meditation amongst the different groups of people is similar. Not only is peace and tranquility fostered, but the meditators are able to manifest whatever it is that they want and become fully aware about everything that surrounds them. This book will concentrate on current meditation practices and the ways in which it will improve your life.

Types of Meditation

There are many different types of meditation, with the two major groups being guided meditation and personally-induced meditation.

First, you must note that there are people who are already experts in meditation and can thus enter into a trance as and when they want. For such people, meditation is as simple as finding a quiet place, sitting down, and guiding their mind for whatever reason they want that day. Since there are many things you can meditate about, such persons have little trouble and can **personally induce** their trance.

For others, whether beginners or experts who cannot bring themselves to control their minds, they may require help from a third party. These types of people require what is known as **guided meditation**. This is the most common type of meditation, and it involves following instruction from an expert. For the guided meditation to work, you must listen to the voice of the instructor only, and follow what you are told to do. If they tell you to take a deep breath, you must take a deep breath. Such instructors then work on getting your mind to a place where it is in a trance, and you can direct the thoughts to whatever you want to focus on. Currently, there are many resources online that offer guided meditation, and physical localities such as the places which offer Yoga classes. Depending on your preferences, you can choose which works best for you.

The following types of meditation can either be achieved through a guided meditation or personal inducement. Each of the meditation types has their own advantages, as illustrated.

1. Mindfulness Meditation

Mindful meditation is one of the best ways to learn

meditation as a beginner. The practice entails being aware of your surroundings and refraining from taking anything for granted. For example, you can start by appreciating nature while you are taking a walk, and even paying attention to something as trivial as the direction the wind is blowing.

One of the best things about mindful meditation is that it can be practiced literally everywhere. You may just be seated in your house and begin listening to the sounds of your surroundings, paying attention to everything you hear. Notably, you must ensure that the room is as silent as possible, and you just need to look around and appreciate everything. Despite the fact that you probably bought everything in your house, you will be surprised at the level to which being conscious of their existence will teach you. To make the meditation even more profound and personalized, move around and touch everything therein, and really pay attention to the details that encompass the furniture as well as their texture. In chapter 2, you will learn about the association of meditation with the overall energies, which will cement the ideology of involving touch in meditation.

Always involve gratitude in your meditations, whichever type you use. In mindful meditation, this helps you appreciate how everything is coordinated in your surroundings, and really puts you in the midst of everything to feel as if you are one. The more you learn about gratitude, the better and more fulfilling meditation will be for you. Let us break down the knowledge into a series of steps that you can easily follow.

Let us analyze the key steps you should follow to become a skilled mindful meditator:

- As has already been stated, the first thing is ensuring that you are in a serene environment. The mind reacts to noise, and if you are not in a quiet place, it may be more difficult for you to concentrate — which means that the meditation process is compromised. However, if you are having a difficult time ignoring the noises that may be surrounding you, there are some meditation sounds that are available online which you can use to help. Such songs are usually either a continuous note of the same intensity, which helps reduce brain activity and puts you in a sort of trance. This is very beneficial.

- The second step is to look around and be fully conscious of your reality. Acknowledge everything as it is, which means that you should not focus on the good aspects only. For instance, if you are out in the field, you can acknowledge that there are some parts of the vegetation which are burned by the sun and there are some parts which are undoubtedly dirty. Also, be attentive and acknowledge how your body reacts to your reality. Some beautiful aspects will fill your heart with joy, while others may make you feel some level of dissatisfaction.

- One very important factor is that you must never

attempt to manipulate or change reality. If something is unsatisfactory, do not try to convince yourself that it is acceptable. Likewise, when something is beautiful, do not come up with negative perceptions, which may make you disregard the beauty. For instance, when you look at a beautiful couple passing by, your immediate thought may be charm and happiness. Do not ruin that thought by shifting to your own dysfunctional relationship. Stay in the moment.

- It is very important to have a main focus point during meditation. For most meditators, the main focus of meditation is breathing. Therefore, you will most likely see practitioners breathing in and out and concentrating on their breath as they take in their surroundings.

- Lastly, always learn to appreciate the present moment.

There are a number of advantages to a person who is adopting the mindful concentration strategy. Some of these key benefits include:

- Mindful meditation is linked with reduced anxiety, depression, and stress. As you can tell from the series of steps, the meditation is primarily inclined toward ensuring you are living in appreciation of the current moment. As is known, some people with depression are dwelling on past activities that may have aggrieved them, while anxiety can be caused by the fear of the unknown, particularly about the future. These end up causing stress, which in turn leads to even more mental dysfunctionalities. When you are meditating mindfully, you are expected to focus on your current situation and surroundings, and not the past nor the future. This focus is imperative in reducing the impacts of those two disorders.

- Also, mindful meditation is known to help practitioners cope with difficult situations without enduring depressing and stressful episodes. You must note that, sometimes, you will undergo some situations that may seemingly break you. If you cannot move on, it becomes even worse for you. When you are meditating mindfully, you are forced to come to terms with your current situation, which means there is no way to ignore what is happening around you. Ultimately, the acceptance of whatever it is that may have happened will help you develop a coping mechanism and, in the process, maintain your sanity.

- More importantly, mindful meditation helps build resilience and confidence. If you are able to control your mind and thoughts, you are stronger than you may even realize, and there is nothing you can't deal with when you put your mind to it.

2. Spiritual Meditation

Spirituality is amongst the primary reasons why people meditate. Almost all religions have an element of spiritual meditation, most of which is disguised under the specific terminology of the various religious groups. Mostly, the spiritual traditions from the east — which encompass Buddhists, Taoists, and Hindus — are the ones most known for in-depth meditation, all of which is aimed at getting them in the same realm as their various spiritual gods.

There are different ways through which spiritual meditation is conducted, and it is evident that each religion is particular to how they want the practice carried out. For instance, the Buddhists usually do basic breath meditation, where they focus on their breathing in a quiet and uplifted place. Worth noting is that Buddhist meditation is very specific, and the practitioners must always sit cross-legged with a straight back, without necessarily supporting themselves on anything. The fundamental element that you must always keep in mind is to ensure you are comfortable and nothing is hurting your back. Once done, the Buddhists conduct the meditation in relation to the specific outcome that they hope to achieve. For instance, some meditate to seek forgiveness, some to instill peace and tranquility in their hearts, and some for reasons as basic as just connecting with their surroundings.

You can compare the serene meditation of the

Buddhists to some of the pagan spiritual groups such as Wicca. Wicca is a group of pagans whose spirituality is inclined toward the invoking of spirits and redirecting their energies as they see fit. The Wiccans also cast magic and spells, although the principal basis of such spells is that it should not result in the harm of others. Usually, the meditation strategy of the Wicca is different in the sense that it is only done to invite the spirits, gods, and the necessary energies as required. The Wicca concentrate on the intent for which they are about to cast the spells and ask the gods to participate.

This is just an illustration of the differences in spiritual meditation, and if you are interested, you will have to approach your religious leaders so they can tell you how they conduct the said meditation.

Mostly, spiritual meditations are carried out at particular places of worship, or at your home if your religious practices allow. Most of these meditations are geared toward spiritual growth and self-reflection, and most of the religious groups mean well when they encourage the growth of such practices. In almost all these meditations, you are required to utter prayers, where you can ask the deity you worship for whatever it is you might wish.

Since spiritual meditation is undoubtedly focused toward the positive growth of a person, some of the key advantages of indulging in it include:

- Spiritual meditations enable you to settle your thoughts and release your emotions. Usually, there is a sense of peace that comes about when you are sure there is someone who has your best interest at heart, and you can cast all your worries and supplications to them. Each spiritual group has a deity, all of whom are considered to be powerful, knowledgeable, and caring. Whenever you meditate, you are releasing everything to them and allowing them to take control. Allah, God, Krishna, and whichever deity you worship is always considered to be listening to you, and believers feel as if a heavy load has been lifted whenever they finish the meditation process. This is good for the body and soul.

- Most spiritual meditation is also inclined toward ensuring believers are focused on the future and not the past. With such a mentality, issues of depression and anxiety are reduced significantly.

- You must realize that the person you are today may not necessarily be the person you were meant to be in the long run. Spiritualism helps connect you to the highest form of self-consciousness, which enables you to become a better person, overall. For example, most religions require you to meditate so as to connect with the deity and seek what you would love to have in the long term. Simply put, the teachings conform to the law of attraction (see chapter 2), which is a form of consciousness that has enabled hundreds of people to grow and develop exponentially in their various undertakings.

- Finally, spiritual meditation allows you to realize there is more to your life than merely the body you are inhabiting. The consciousness about the available power around you is one of the factors which causes an increased level of what is known as self-realization.

3. Focused meditation

Focused meditation is considered to be amongst the practices which have significantly helped enable people to build their mental agility. The meditative practice involves a total and undeterred focus on a particular subject matter, regardless of how trivial it may be. The difference between focused meditation and other meditative practices is that you do not have to be in a quiet environment for the former. Also, you are not required to be still, and you can go ahead with the primary activities you would normally do without any problem. The fundamental goal of the meditation is to ensure that you build the ability to focus on a task unabated, and that you can carry on without constantly fidgeting or getting distracted by other things.

Some of the people who employ the focused meditation strategy are athletes, musicians, and individual performers in their different capacities. The meditation is critical, mainly when the act you are performing requires a considerable amount of time and concentration. For instance, most soulful pianists, guitarists, and violinists express total concentration whenever they are playing their instruments. It is common to see such people quiet, with their eyes closed — not even the claps and cheering distracts them from their process of playing. Athletes, most notably long-distance runners, are also advised to develop focused meditation. When they master the practice, it becomes effortless to concentrate on the goal of running many miles without focusing on aspects such as how hot or cold it is, how tired they are, and even self-defeating thoughts that may tell them they cannot achieve what it is they are seeking.

In all honesty, achieving focused meditation is one of the simplest yet hardest tasks. Human beings have been conditioned to the belief that they have to multi-task to get their work done, which is a very misleading ideology. Even if you are involved in multiple activities, the fact remains that you only have two hands and that at each particular time, you will be handling one task. When you realize how unsatisfying, tiring, and mind-scattering the practice of multi-tasking can be, you will be better suited to embrace focused meditation.

The following are some of the procedures that you can try out at each particular time to develop focus.

- Regardless of the amount of work you need to complete on your to-do-list, ensure that you focus on one task at a time. There is usually more fulfillment when you finish the tasks in their entirety and tick them off the list.

- Realize no task is as trivial as it may seem. If you

are taking a cup of tea, put everything else aside. Do not check your phone while in the process, and do not visit the various social media sites on your computer. Concentration is concentration, and all tasks must be given the attention that they deserve. Keep in mind that, even when you are performing actions such as taking a cup of tea, your mind should be on that tea. Notice the scent and aroma of the drink, the level of heat, the texture of the cup, and the most basic flavors you may have typically overlooked. Appreciate how the tea tastes, and how warm it makes your body one sip after the other. In the beginning, this may be very difficult. However, bring your mind back when it wanders.

As you may have noted, the focused type of meditation is more like mindfulness meditation, only this type teaches you how to actually focus on a single task 100%. There are undoubted benefits from mastering this type of meditation, some of which include:

- Focused meditation is one of the contributors to increased efficiency, which is a result of focusing on a single task and ensuring there are minimal distractions. It is said that whenever your focus is on the optimum, it is improbable that you will fall prey to some of the time-wasting, inefficient practices such as procrastination and uncompleted tasks.

- Also, the focused meditation technique helps when it comes to the improvement of the different senses in the body. For instance, when you concentrate on the taste of the food as well as the smell of the things that surround you, you influence your body to be more aware and receptive of such senses, which ultimately makes them advance and develop.

- More importantly, a decluttered mind is peaceful and tranquil. There is some level of anxiety that comes from handling too many tasks at once, since many of them are often left uncompleted. When you focus on single tasks, you not only complete them more efficiently and ultimately tick them off your list, but you also manage to do so with little to no anxiety.

4. Visualization Meditation

Visualization meditation is one of the most transformational techniques that have helped people improve in various aspects of their lives. This meditation requires full attention as well as focus, and you are required to have a mental picture of the things you wish to achieve. For people who are enthusiastic about the law of attraction and such, the visualization technique is ideal.

To explain briefly how the visualization technique works, note that you must be at a level where you are conscious about the different things that are available in the world, ranging from different energies to the degree to which the mind plays a role in the extent of success and development that you achieve. The basic principle that resonates with the visualization technique is that whatever the mind can perceive is not out of reach, and can be achieved. For that reason, most of the people who use visualization meditation are those who are interested in manifesting something into their lives. These manifestations are not limited to any particular thing and can range from personal possessions to more intrinsic needs such as companionship and love.

To explain how strong the visualization technique is, we shall consider the group that is mostly known for its usage, which is the Wiccan pagans. The Wiccans are known as witches by some people, since they participate in events ranging from the casting of spells to conducting magic.

For instance, let us assume that a Wiccan witch wants to conduct a healing spell. As they meditate on the spell and the intent to which they are invoking the gods, the pagans will actually visualize the disease leaving the body of the afflicted person, and they will ensure that there is no doubt within them that they will achieve their intent. Most of the spells cast by Wiccans come to pass, and it is all through the power of visual meditation and belief concerning the associating inference.

To some people, visual meditation provides a necessary escape from the world. For instance, you may be at the lowest point in your life, feeling that nothing good can ever come out of the situation in which you find yourself. Most people rely on pain medications and seek comfort from the people around them. For those who know the power of visual meditation, however, this is their escape.

Different things will evoke different feelings for you. For example, whenever you think about the beautiful beach, you may have an increased sense of happiness. For some people, thinking about their family or pet can instantly put them in a good mood. To embrace the visual meditation process, it is essential to identify what makes you tick so you can use it whenever you need an escape. In the situation illustrated above, assuming that your pet is a contributor to your happiness, you can be intentional and focus on only the memory and picture of him, even as you lie on a hospital bed. Visualize him running to you, playing, or go back to a time when you felt incredibly happy. If you can achieve total concentration on that vision, you will have escaped temporarily from the reality of your situation, and even those few minutes of relief are beneficial.

Visualization meditation has the highest number of benefits, and they include:

- It helps in the improvement of performance. According to Daniel Kadish, a New York psychologist, you can use visualization to prepare for any kind of event in your life. Most professionals use imagery, particularly doctors and surgeons, as they prepare for complicated procedures. There is power in visualizing those parts of the body and how you are going to conduct the operation to ensure that no errors are made in the process. In this case, visualization plays the role of practicing.

- Reduction of stress. Visual meditation allows people to focus on the things that are functioning well and whatever is going right, as opposed to whatever may be going wrong. Whenever you have good thoughts, feel-good hormones (endorphins) are released. The more endorphins are released, the better your mood will be, which means there will be no place for the stress to continue disturbing you.

- Whenever you are visualizing something, there is an improvement to your level of focus and concentration, which will help you carry out different tasks with efficiency.

- It boosts confidence and morale. In the world of visualization, nothing is impossible. We will look at how meditation influences the subconscious mind in the following chapter, to explain why so many favorable inferences emanate from the simple procedure of sitting down and "fantasizing." As you imagine yourself excelling, it becomes imprinted in your brain that you are capable of achieving anything, which is then reflected in your confidence and general demeanor.

- Visualization meditation has been known to heal even the sickest of patients. Also, meditation is a natural pain reliever, and you may hear people talk about hypnotherapy in the relieving of pain that medication failed to achieve. This is also something to do with the programming of the mind, which is discussed in depth in chapter 2.

- You will become more creative. The ultimate benefit of meditation is increased creativity. As you begin to create mental images and visualize objects, the mind becomes highly invigorated. Therefore, the development of all the senses means you will ultimately become more creative and you will have the ability to draw into more vivid descriptions and achieve more explicit focus and awareness of the things around you.

Chapter 2: Meditation and its Influence on the Mind

You must have heard these popular phrases that all relate to the power of the brain:

"Whatever the mind can perceive can be achieved."

"Prosperity begins when you tune your brain to focus on what you want to achieve."

"Whatever a man asks for, he shall receive."

"Whatever a man thinks he is, that is the exact thing that he is"

All of these phrases point to the power of the mind. While we all agree with the sayings and affirm that, indeed, there is a need to change the way we think and view ourselves, what exactly are we talking about? We are talking about the unmatched power of the brain.

Before we begin to understand how meditation influences our brains, let us start by understanding that the brain has three primary parts: the conscious, unconscious, and subconscious.

Conscious Mind

The conscious mind is what is primarily regarded as the brain, which is responsible for our current awareness. At this particular point, you are aware of yourself, your feelings, your thoughts, everything that is surrounding you, and any noises that are within your sensory scope. The conscious mind represents what people associate you with, which means that it is the part that gives you your personality and decision-making capability to govern how you react to different situations. Whenever you look at a person and decide to smile at them, greet them, or hug them, it is all thanks to the present consciousness, which is made possible by the conscious mind.

The conscious mind communicates with the outside world, through speech, writing, drawings, and various forms of artistic work. To oneself, the conscious mind will communicate through thoughts and realizations.

Unconscious Mind

As we go about the daily activities in our lives, we meet many different people, some of whom stay in our lives while some we lose touch with. Also, there are millions of occurrences happening to us each day, some of which are repetitive while some of which are new. The human being has the capability to store information in the form of data in our brain, although some of this information ends up being stored in a part of the brain known as the unconscious level. At this moment, you may not vividly remember a topic you learned two years ago. However, when you go through the book again, you realize a sense of familiarity, which means the information is not new to you. Once you read it, you remember what you learned, and there is a higher chance you may retain the data compared to a person who has just learned it for the very first time. This is due to the fact that the memory was not erased, but was instead stored in this part of the brain.

Notably, since the information is still present in the brain, it will, in most cases, be communicated to the conscious using the subconscious as the vessel. It is for this reason that you are highly likely to dream about an event that happened to you ten years ago and remember it when you finally wake up — particularly where traumatic events were involved, such as falling from a significant height, breaking limbs, and traumatic accidents.

The Subconscious Mind

The subconscious mind is undoubtedly one of the most exciting parts of the brain. To some people, this part of the brain can be likened to computer RAM. Typically, the subconscious is responsible for the storage of recent memories and is considered to play a significant role in how a person behaves and responds to the different things that may come his way. Everything, including some of your patterns and behaviors that may seem trivial like sleeping and waking up, is all encrypted on the subconscious mind. It is worth noting that the subconscious part is considered to be the part of the brain that has the most awareness. In simple terms, when we talk about the "sixth sense," we are referring to the information revealed by the subconscious mind.

So, how does meditation interact with the various parts of the brain?

First things first, it is worth noting that only two parts of the brain are involved in the meditation process — the conscious and subconscious parts. The role of the conscious part of the brain is minimal, since all it is required to do is make the decision to meditate, and prepare everything that is needed to start the process.

When you begin meditating, note that while you may think it is just reflecting on the conscious level, it is actually much more profound. Meditation broadly touches upon the subconscious mind and influences the resultant outcomes.

Consider this:

There are many problems that are deeply rooted in our bodies whose answer lies in the connection to the subconscious mind. The subconscious mind is considered to be the life-ward of the body, which means that whichever decisions and inferences made regarding the pivotal aspects of our lives all relate to the condition of this part of our minds. There are certain body functions that are regulated by the subconscious mind, which includes breathing in and out, homeostasis, maintenance of blood pressure, and even the digestive process. What many people may not understand is that our ability to prosper, live a positive and well-defined life, and perform and behave in a certain way are also all dependent on the level to which we are able to rewire our subconscious mind.

This is where it gets interesting

The conscious mind can distinguish between things and acts that have occurred from those that have not. Therefore, when I tell you that a blue car has arrived, you can be almost sure that a blue car has arrived. However, the subconscious mind is different. This part cannot distinguish between various things, which means it relies on what you feed it. Through meditation, you get to feed it whatever it is that you wish. The trouble with this phenomenon is that it can either propel you towards greatness or leave you in a destitute state. You've surely heard of the common phrase that what you think you are is what you are. This subconscious part of the brain is what is mostly responsible for determining what a person becomes in the end, hence the need to restructure it in a more positive manner.

To really get what we mean by the subconscious mind influencing the overall person and what they become, we can take the example of the law of attraction.

Law of Attraction

The law of attraction is based on the simple ideology that we are responsible for all the things we attract into our lives. Therefore, in this world which has endless and limitless possibilities, each of us has the capability to be whatever we would want to be in life. All you need to do is to attract what you want through the basic act of focusing and guiding the energies which you believe are the root to whatever it is that you wish to achieve.

Notably, the law of attraction is governed by your ability to harness the collective power of your mind — most particularly the subconscious mind. All our thoughts are capable of becoming our reality, which is why people who focus on failure tend to experience failure more often than those who are more inclined towards positivity. Basically, the law is based on the notion that if your attention is on gloom and bad energy, there is a possibility that you will always attract these negative energies into your life. Consequently, if you are all about positivity and positive energy, you are likely to attract the best into your life.

The idea is that we all have the capability of creating our own sunshine, as well as achieving anything we could have ever dreamed of. This is why the law of attraction is considered to be the most powerful law, universally. Basically, each person is in a constant state of creation, which means you are always creating your own reality and future from your own thoughts and mentality. For that reason, you must always be very careful about what is going through your mind, whether it is conscious or subconscious. The sooner you realize that thoughts determine what goes on in our lives, the more you will strive to actually create the thoughts that are empowering and beneficial to you as a person.

Everything in the universe is matter, which is made from energy. As you know, energy is never constant — therefore, the vibrations that we either send out or receive are always moving. You may hear people talk about positive energy, or doing away with negative energy. What this means is that we realize that there can be both good and bad energy around us, and it is up to our actions to determine the type of energies that we shall face. When you are in a state of happiness, fulfillment, peace, and kindness, you will be sending out positive energy. Likewise, if you are in a constant state of negativity, disharmony, resentment, anger, and pride, you will be sending out negative energy.

Whatever you send out will always find its way back to you. When you send out positivity, it comes back to you — and so does negativity. Those vibrations are sent out to the universe. Since you attract what you are, these thoughts are part of you and you are basically asking the universe for more of the same. Through meditation, you can ensure that you send out the absolute best vibrations possible.

Meditation and the Law of Attraction

As you have learned, the law of attraction reacts to the various thoughts we have, and subsequently ensures that our thoughts become our reality. Therefore, our mind acts as a magnet and amplifier, where what you are feeling is amplified regardless of whether it is good or bad. Therefore, you must be very cautious about what you allow to dwell in your mind. One of the best ways through which you can change this outcome is through meditation and ensuring that all your thoughts represent the best version of both who you are and what you aspire to be.

You can use any type of meditation to influence the law of attraction, although visual meditation and mindfulness are some of the best strategies to influence how you feel. As was stated earlier, the law of attraction and meditation greatly influences the subconscious mind, which means that they determine the reactions and energies that result from such interactions. It's important to keep in mind that the subconscious mind is easily deceived. Usually, this part of the mind has no way of distinguishing between reality and a façade. For this reason, you must manipulate it and enjoy the positive inferences that ensue.

Meditation entails positivity. You are only supposed to dwell on the things that stir a good feeling within you. Whatever you visualize — whether it is a lake, beach, or your family — to escape from the stresses of the world, the subconscious mind considers this to be a reality, and the result is that the feelings created manifest outwardly. No matter how you feel, if you visualize and focus on positivity, the subconscious will believe that, indeed, you are happy, and the result will be the release of the feel-good hormones responsible for dealing with depression, anxiety, and even pain.

Likewise, whenever you are meditating and visualizing the positivity of the world, you are sending out positive energy and vibes into the world. These positives will ultimately come back to you, and you will be surrounded by good energy. As the common saying goes, this world is a mirror and whatever you give, you will get back in return.

Now that you already know about the law of attraction, here are a series of steps you can easily follow, and soon you will be manifesting everything you ever needed into your life.

The first step is to **determine the position** at which you are most comfortable while beginning the meditation. Some people like to lie on their backs, preferably in a soft place such as a bed; others may prefer outdoors surrounded by green vegetation, and others may just prefer to use the millennial strategy of using a yoga mat and taking a yoga pose. Here, the main thing you must consider is comfort.

Once you have taken your preferred position, the next step involves **focusing on your intent.** It may be that you would like to manifest something into your life, or get rid of a feeling, ideology, or notion that no longer serves you. If you desire to manifest something, you must be clear on exactly what it is — whether a job, career success, peace, or anything else you may be focused on achieving at that particular time. Once you have your intent established, you can meditate and manifest literally anything that you may wish.

As you start focusing on your intent, in most cases, you will recognize **some opposing thoughts and limiting beliefs**, which we commonly refer to as logic. These thoughts will attempt to show you why whatever it is that you are seeking is invalid, and why you cannot achieve this. No matter how logical and true these beliefs seem, acknowledge them, and **disregard them completely**. If you allow them to thrive, you will begin looking for the reasons why whatever it is that you are seeking will not work, ultimately limiting and inhibiting yourself.

Visualize what you want to manifest. If it is a career, picture yourself actually walking into an office and working at your desk. If it is getting well, visualize yourself walking on a beach or any other happy place without a single pain in your body. When it comes to visualization, human beings were gifted with the highest level of imagination and creativity. That means there is not one object of visualization that is out of bounds for anyone. If you can dream and visualize it, you can achieve it.

Finally, you need to change your mental status — you need to start **acting like a person who has already received what they are manifesting**. If you wanted financial stability, begin acting like a person who has their finances in order. If you want better health, begin acting like a person who is already feeling better. Avoid limiting talk at all times. When you manage to trick the subconscious mind into believing that you are in a certain place, you will send out the energies more efficiently, and you can be sure that they will come back with results.

What Meditation is Not

Now that you have all the basics of meditations, we need to demystify what it is not. There are some people, mostly beginners, who make the mistake of associating meditation with incorrect notions from the onset and ultimately make huge mistakes. Some of the common associations include:

1. Thinking

In as much as meditation is normally carried out silently, it is not about thinking. Whenever you are consciously thinking, you are often not settled on any one particular topic, and thoughts are considered to be a summary of cluttered and disorganized ideologies. The human brain is capable of developing up to 2,000 thoughts in a minute, and some of them you may not even realize since they are handled by the subconscious mind. For instance, when you are walking around your house and make the right corner to go to the bedroom, it may seem obvious. However, the eyes have coordinated with the brain and legs and decided that it is logical for you to make a right turn since turning left would have taken you somewhere else. These thoughts, and other more conscious ones, are not meditations.

Whenever you meditate, you must focus on a particular theme and try to close out any other thought. If you are visualizing yourself on a beach, keep your thoughts focused on that particular direction and refrain from any wandering thoughts. It is difficult to stop the brain from processing any other thoughts, and one of the techniques that works well is acknowledging these thoughts and letting them go.

Meditation is often related to a positive focus. Therefore, you cannot spend two hours thinking about something that has hurt you, or a bad situation that you may be in, and claim that you have been meditating. That is merely thinking about your problems, and it will not help you achieve the results that meditation does. If you are indeed in a troubling situation, the best meditation technique would be for you to focus on what is working, and attempt to attract a better situation through manifestation. If you do not have money, start meditating about abundance. If you are sick, meditate about tranquility and good health.

Note, this should not amount to wishful thinking. When you meditate, you should be so deeply indulged into your visualization that the body will feel as if you have already obtained what you wish to have. If your idea of meditation is just stressing or tiring you out, then you are likely overthinking. When you meditate right, you will be in a position of absolute peace and tranquility, and you will emerge refreshed and invigorated.

2. Daydreaming

The fact that you are supposed to visualize things that do not exist in the present moment does not mean that meditation is merely daydreaming. Often, daydreaming is related to fantasy in the sense that whatever you are focusing on cannot happen in the real world. Most young girls daydream about being queens and princesses when they grow up, something that can never happen. You can also fantasize about someone and spend hours thinking about them. Celebrities are amongst the people who are fantasized about the most by their fans, some of whom wish they were married to them and others may wish that they were part of their families and acquaintances. Yes, you may have locked out all other thoughts and concentrated on these celebrities. Yes, the daydreaming offers an escape from the reality of the world. But this is not meditation. As we have discussed, meditation is inclined upon the things that are actually possible, regardless of whether or not they are a stretch. When I meditate about financial security, I may not have a way out at the moment, but I know that it is possible with a shift in my activities or increased hard work. Consequently, meditating about better health is reasonable and achievable, unlike the

Prince Charming one might daydream about.

3. Chanting Affirmations

I will begin by saying that affirmations and meditations are closely related, and they can be used together to achieve a certain purpose. However, the speaking of affirmations is not considered to be meditation in the least. So, what are affirmations?

The term "affirmations" mean to affirm, which is to cement something — in this case, onto ourselves[2]. Everything we say out aloud amounts to affirmations, and the main idea is that when you say something repetitively, you affirm it and it becomes part of you. For example, when you say the following words:

"I am blessed."

"I am healed."

"I am prosperous."

These three chants are an example of what affirmations are all about. As you can see, affirmations are very personal, and that is why the people who chant them include the "I" part to illustrate that they are talking

---

[2] Downing, C. J. (1986). affirmations: steps to counter negative, self-fulfilling prophecies. *Elementary School Guidance & Counseling*, 20(3), 174-179.

about themselves. The main idea behind repeating affirmations over and over again is to get to the point where the mind actually believes what you are saying, and acts in accordance with where you are mentally. The act is considered to be like planting a flower — when you water the plants and nurture them continuously, they will undoubtedly grow. On the other hand, if you neglect them, they will die. Affirmations water the soul by continuously and positively crediting it, ultimately improving your overall mood and ensuring that the image you have of yourself is as positive as possible.

As is evident, when you are making affirmations, you are not focusing on a particular subject matter. Since affirmations are usually short, they only briefly point out to a situation and are not in-depth. However, affirmations are great and very positive when combined with the meditation process. After you are done meditating and filling your world with positivity, chant some of the affirmations five or ten times to affirm what you have meditated upon. For example, if you were meditating on good health and aiming at making a quick recovery, end the meditation by affirming "I am healed," or "I have good health," or however you wish to phrase the affirmation.

4. Praying

Most people who misunderstand meditation confuse it with prayer. Just to reiterate, the one thing that makes meditation unique is the intent of the meditator. When someone is praying, their main focus is connecting to their deity — God, Allah, Buddha, Wicca gods, whoever they are accustomed to. Prayer is more like a conversation, where you are talking with the higher power. When you are praying, it is with the belief that the deity is listening, and that they are capable of granting whatever supplications you may have. Therefore, the prayers are not focused on yourself, but on the highest supreme. This is very different from meditating, which involves talking to oneself and encouraging yourself without the involvement of the higher power. When you meditate, you are talking to yourself — talking to your soul.

Also, the focus of prayers never changes. It is always the Supreme Being, regardless of the situation. When you want a job, you involve your deity to intercede and lead the way for you. When you are sick, you invoke the deity to heal you. In meditation, the focus changes with each of your desires to attract and manifest, and you do not invoke anyone to intercede on your behalf.

Benefits of Meditation

We have looked at some of the benefits of individual meditation techniques only. Notably, there are some benefits that apply to all the meditative techniques used, regardless of the specific type of meditation you decide to use. Some of these benefits include:

1. Promotion of Emotional Health

In a recent study done on 4,600 adults, meditation ranked amongst the top contributors to the promotion of emotional health. Some forms of meditation, such as visualization, enable a person to focus on what they can potentially achieve, which puts you on the forefront toward better emotional stability. The study followed up with 18 participants who began meditating at a time when they struggled with their emotional well-being and experienced increased feelings of low self-esteem and self-worth. The research took place over an extended period of time, and the participants continued meditating over a period of three years. The volunteers underwent various tests within those three years, and the results showed that their levels of depression and anxiety were significantly dropping over the course of that time. By the end of the period, all were considered to be emotionally stable, and their depressive episodes were gone.

The scientific explanation of this reaction emanated from the understanding that the body is constantly producing hormones in relation to impulses sent to the brain. When you are under stress, the body identifies impulses similar to those when you are in trouble. The main chemicals released are cytokines, which are meant to make you more aware in case you may need to get out of a dangerous situation. The release of this chemical not only increases inflammation in the body, but also adversely affects your mood, and the continued release of the same is partly responsible for symptoms of depression.

The more you meditate, the lower your stress levels will be and, consequently, the lower your body's production of such chemicals[3]. Therefore, not only will you be in a better mood, but the feel-good hormone endorphins will be released to help keep any potential depressive episodes at bay. Your improved positivity and view of life will also make you more receptive to the people around you, and having a peaceful correlation with everyone is amongst the ways through which your mental health is facilitated.

2. Increased Self-Awareness

As you may have noticed, the act of meditation helps you to be more conscious and aware of the things around you, and those which influence the various parts of your life. You may not realize it until you try it, but there are very many factors in your life that may seem trivial and, to a larger extent, even meaningless. However, when you consciously decide to be mindful of them, your full

---

[3] Balázs, J., Miklósi, M., Keresztény, Á., Hoven, C. W., Carli, V., Wasserman, C., ... & Cotter, P. (2013). Adolescent subthreshold-depression and anxiety: Psychopathology, functional impairment and increased suicide risk. *Journal of child psychology and psychiatry*, 54(6), 670-677.

understanding and view of life changes.

For example, you may pass through a lawn, forest, or even a park, but not pay attention to any nature found therein. Sometimes, you may be engrossed in social media on your phone or listening to music, which keeps you from focusing on what is around you. The minute you make a conscious effort to begin meditating and becoming conscious of your surroundings, you will be shocked at how deeply engrossing it can be. You will view nature as it really is — how the leaves are blown by the wind, their sizes, shapes, color, texture, and many other things. Being one with your surroundings is very calming, and will give you a feeling of satisfaction by just allowing you to enjoy nature and marvel at how awesome creation is. The ensuing gratitude and satisfaction are amongst the therapies that will enable you to develop your self-awareness.

Also, this self-awareness is in line with the thoughts and individual beliefs we have. Whenever you meditate and focus on a particular subject matter, you will find the clarity you may be seeking about what exactly is happening and why some of these occurrences are happening to you. Also, you develop an increased awareness about some of your more self-defeating thoughts, and how you can prevent them from being a part of your life. This awareness is necessary, and it will guide you toward ensuring that, henceforth, all your talk and action are gearing you in the right direction. Further, you are more likely to develop constructive patterns from the same.

More importantly, the self-awareness garnered through meditation is pivotal in developing a system of creative problem-solving. When you focus deeply on some of the issues in your life, you give your mind the opportunity to find solutions to the problem. For instance, if your focus is on your state of financial instability, this can help you identify the causes of the situation and ways to foster actual change.

3. Helps Improve your Attention Span

Meditation involves focusing on a single issue at a time. The more you train your mind to concentrate on individual issues, the easier it becomes to focus on other things outside of meditation. This training can be likened to exercising your muscles, where the more the resistance you use, the stronger the muscles become.

In our corporate and day-to-day lives, there are some tasks which require us to concentrate for hours. For instance, if you are a short-hand secretary, you will be required to record the minutes of a meeting from the time it starts to when it ends. The meeting may be as short as ten minutes or it could last for hours. If you don't have a good attention span, there is no way you can complete the task efficiently. This is similar to long-distance runners and other athletes — they have to be fixated on a particular means and their attention must not shift, or they will follow through to the end. If a runner starts concentrating on how long the journey is, they may give up midway. But when they focus solely being completing the race, regardless of the challenges, chances are higher that they will succeed.

If you are a student who attends long lectures, meditation is definitely for you. The trained mind will ensure you have no more problems paying attention to your tutor, which is the best way to improve your grades and effectively plan the direction your future will take.

4. Helps in the Control of Anxiety

Anxiety is a common emotion that causes people to be overly concerned about the various things that may be happening to them. One of the major signs of anxiety is increased fear, alertness, and caution. People who are diagnosed with an anxiety disorder have panic attacks, most of which are considered to be unfounded[4]. Anxiety causes increased terror, and the fact that the spasms can be triggered by the slightest of things makes the condition difficult to manage. Most of the people who have panic attacks related to anxiety choose to get prescriptions, which is not a permanent solution in the

---

[4] Balázs, J., Miklósi, M., Keresztény, Á., Hoven, C. W., Carli, V., Wasserman, C., ... & Cotter, P. (2013). Adolescent subthreshold-depression and anxiety: Psychopathology, functional impairment and increased suicide risk. *Journal of child psychology and psychiatry*, *54*(6), 670-677.

long run.

One of concerns regarding the regular use of medication is that anxiety is more of an innate problem than an illness which can be fixed using medication. Most medications produce artificial levels of the feel-good hormones, meaning anxiety sufferers are unable to deal with the root of the problem, and in some cases, end up addicted or dependent on such medications[5].

Meditation, on the other hand, requires you to deal with the experiences that you are undergoing and face them face on. When you meditate, you attain a level of personal consciousness that you may previously not have known was possible. As a result, you have the opportunity to deal with all of the issues that affect you and achieve total healing. Since meditation is geared towards positivity, you are better able to ease any fears and worries that may have weighed you down previously, and making a full recovery very easy.

5. Helps in Improving Memory

We have already discussed the conscious, subconscious, and unconscious part of the brain. As we learned, the unconscious part of the brain is the segment which holds all our memories, right from childhood to the

---

[5] Spielberger, C. D. (Ed.). (2013). *Anxiety: Current trends in theory and research.* Elsevier.

present day. This information is not easily accessible, but it mostly manifests to the conscious mind using the subconscious mind as a ladder.

The mind is a large muscle, and just like with any other muscle in the body, the more you exercise it, the stronger it will get. Meditation is considered to be amongst the best exercises for the brain, which means that the more you meditate, the stronger your mental agility. This exercise usually benefits all the parts of the brain, which means you will have an easier time accessing memories that you may have thought were lost. Also, since meditation is mainly inclined toward reaching the subconscious mind and reformatting it, the result is that the conscious mind will be able to easily reach the immediate memories stored therein. The unconscious part will also have a better and stronger ladder, and you will be capable of remembering more information than you ever thought possible.

As your mental health becomes stronger, you will have a lower risk of developing ailments such as dementia and memory loss. Regardless of your genes or family heritage, strengthening your mind is one of the best bets to ensure that you do not end up suffering from such ailments.

6. Helps in Generating Kindness

Meditation puts you in a good mood. When you are in a good mood, you are more likely to be kind and nice to the people around you. Similar to the saying that people who are hurt are likely to hurt others, the people who are kind to themselves are likely to be kind to other people, as well. With more practice, you will realize that as you extend love and kindness toward yourself, so will you to the other people around you, too.

7. Helps in the Fighting of Addictions

One of the greatest lessons you learn when meditating is self-discipline. If you can effectively focus your mind on a particular thing and refrain from diverting your attention, it is likely you can exert that control in any area of your life. With that self-control come other positive traits such as awareness and decisiveness.

Addictions are part of the habits that people often think that they have no control over. Most drug and substance addicts affirm that they may have tried to stop their habits in the past, but were unable due to the demands of the body. As such people say, the desire was stronger than their restraint.

When you finally manage to control your mind, emotions, and thoughts, you can easily fight the urges that define any type of addiction you may have. Learning to shift the thoughts in your mind means that you can shift your desires from those destructive substances to healthier options. Notably, meditators succeed more than any other group of people when it comes to weight loss, since they are able to focus on the goal and practice discipline.

8. Helps Improve Sleep

The use of meditation to promote sleep is a personal favorite. As a beginner, it is recommended to adopt the guided meditation if your intention is to fall asleep. Experts can invoke meditative episodes by themselves to quiet the mind and fall asleep. If you use guided meditation, you need to pay attention to the leader and do everything they tell you to. This guided meditation works like hypnosis, where the narrator is able to reach your subconscious mind and put you to sleep in no time.

Anybody can use meditation to sleep, particularly insomniacs. The technique is very safe, and even small children can use it with no problems.

Chapter 3: Step-by-Step Guide to Meditation

What You Need Before Meditating

Meditation is one of the most straightforward practices that you can ever do. As an aspiring meditator, there are only two things you will need before you are well on your way to begin your practice.

1. An Identified Personal Space

In the previous sections, we affirmed that meditation is not very strict and you can literally begin meditating from anywhere, both indoors and out. However, if your intention is to be a constant and regular meditator, you may want to identify a spot and space that will best work for you, to ensure that the mind automatically enters the meditative mode when you approach that space. This is comparable to a person going to church or any other place of worship — whenever you approach that space, your brain automatically adjusts and prepares for spiritualism and connecting with the deity.

When you are meditating, you are focused on connecting with yourself. Since meditation is a very personal process, there is a need to have personal space, as well. For some people, space may be on their balcony, bedroom, living room, garden, or virtually any other place which provides the tranquility and peace needed to carry out the meditation effectively.

Once you have identified the space, you then need to place your meditation materials therein. Some of these materials include:

- A chair for the people who concentrate better when they are sitting upright while supported at the back. Ensure the chair is as comfortable as possible to prevent issues such as aggravated back problems and pains. There is no restriction to the types of chairs that can be used — use the one that makes you feel the most comfortable.

- Meditation cushions. The meditation cushions are for the people who have no problem sitting upright without support. Experts use the cushions in most cases and the fact that you have to consciously ensure that you remain upright and do not topple over means you will have elevated levels of alertness. Ultimately, the quality of your meditation improves.

- Meditation mat. The meditation mats are basically the same as those used for yoga, which are flat and soft. Just like the cushions, these mats are for people who can comfortably sit upright without causing harm to their backs.

- Pillow. Some people concentrate better when they are lying on their backs, which makes the meditation more effective when they are either on their beds or are laying elsewhere. Make sure that your head is comfortable, especially if you are outdoors and are laying on the grass or on a flat surface. Safety is always the first priority, and you should avoid laying down in places you are not absolutely sure about.

For beginners, I would recommend the use of chairs and benches with back support for the first few sessions, then gradually shift to meditation mats and cushions.

2. A Timer

It's a good idea to use a timer while carrying out your meditation. These can take many different forms, from a phone to an actual timer. The key benefit to using a timer is that they help you program your time efficiently, which means that you will be able to keep track of the length of time you want to carry out the meditation.

As you become more acquainted with meditation, you will be able to control the duration of the meditation time more efficiently and you will have no problems meditating over a defined period of time. At this point, you are ready to begin meditation.

Key Pointers to Keep in Mind During Meditation

As you begin meditating, there are a number of things you should keep in mind. Go through this list carefully before you begin meditating for some tips which will help you easily go through the meditation process with little worry.

1. The mind cannot go blank, even when you are meditating. There is a common misconception that during meditation, the mind should go blank. That couldn't be further from the truth. There is no particular time that the mind can go blank — you are bound to realize some random thoughts passing through the brain, even as you intently focus on a particular subject. When you experience these unrelated thoughts, acknowledge them and let them go. Thoughts should not disrupt your meditation process.

2. There is no particular posture for proper meditation. When people think about meditation, there is a common association of sitting down, legs crossed and hands stretched out. While this is one of the sitting positions that many meditators use, it is not the only one. Meditation just requires you to be in a position of comfort — it does not matter whether you are sitting down in a chair, lying on your back, or standing.

Whatever feels most comfortable to you is how you should practice.

3. There is no specific guideline that pertains to the meditation process, and you can learn through multiple processes. Currently, many people are acquainted with the meditation practice, and you can learn through scholars, books, trainers, online, and any other source available to you.

4. Do not take the process too seriously. Meditation should be relaxing and not add to your stress. If your practice tires you out and half of the time you aren't even sure what you're doing, it is a sign that you are meditating the wrong way altogether. Try to concentrate on a particular topic, but refrain from acts of aggression, desperation, and feelings of hopelessness if you cannot achieve what you are seeking.

5. There are many health benefits of meditation. That said, ensure that you also do what is necessary to promote the faster manifestation of this good health. For example, if you are dealing with some sort of addiction, no level of meditation can make the addiction go away if you are still indulging in various drugs. Likewise, you cannot meditate acne away if you are still eating unhealthy junk foods. Inner harmony and energy must always be in line with the external. The more you follow up the meditation with conscious activities, the better the manifestation will be.

6. Meditation is more mainstream than you think. Some people may believe meditation is something that has

recently been developed, but meditation is an ancient practice that was developed many centuries ago. Meditative techniques were used in the fostering of inner peace as well as mitigating pain.

7. You can never be too busy for meditation. Meditation is dynamic and flexible, which means that you can practice it for five minutes, ten minutes, or one hour or more — whatever duration you prefer. The fact that you can even meditate when you are walking and when you are just about to sleep means that there is always a chance you can fit it in your schedule whenever possible. A typical person can spend hours on social media and entertainment sites such as Netflix. Therefore, you can choose whichever time you want to relax and slide in some quick meditation.

8. Meditation is considered to be just like exercise. Therefore, even if you do not get it right the first time, you can always keep practicing. Think of meditation like a person working out in a gym to reduce their weight. The weight loss does not happen overnight, but when they keep up with the practice, the pounds gradually drop. The more you meditate, the better you become.

9. Once you are done meditating, always take a step back and evaluate how you feel after the practice. If you felt more at peace and energized, you can be sure that you are meditating the right way. If you feel worse off than when you began, there is a high chance that you are just overthinking, which means you need to revisit your meditation techniques.

How to Meditate Like a Pro

The following is a two-week instructional guide, assuming that you will be meditating at least five days each week. Follow this guide step by step, and you will be well on your way to becoming an expert. Before we begin, it is important to note that there are many ways and approaches that you can take to learn meditation, and this is just one of them.

Day 1: Metta Meditation

The first day of meditation should be inclined toward ensuring that you are the best version of yourself. One of the major ways through which you can achieve this higher self is through the attraction of positivity and beneficial influences into your life in a manner known as Metta meditation. The term Metta refers to a loving and kind relationship, which is considered to be both unconditional and wise. This love has no strings attached, and is considered to be exclusive — one of the most real forms of love that a person can ever get. Before you extend this kind of love to other people, you must ensure you have already given it to yourself.

You cannot give what you do not have. In meditation, the main goal is always to improve our relationship with ourselves, which will also manifest in how we relate to the people around us. If we have not cultivated this love within ourselves, there is no way that we can show such love to others, including our family and friends. When you succeed in the Metta meditation, the rate at which you will grow and develop mentally will motivate you to follow through with the other types of meditations.

The Procedure for Carrying out the Metta Meditation

The first step is to prepare the area and specific place where you will carry out the meditation. If you choose to sit on a chair, pillow, or a mat, ensure that you have already placed these in the place where you wish to meditate. The most important thing is to ensure that you are not carrying out the meditation out of obligation, but that you wish to enjoy the benefits that emanate from the process. Once you get your intent right, you are definitely ready to begin.

If you are sitting on a bench or a chair, ensure that you are comfortable with your feet on the floor while your spine remains straight. If you are on a mat or cushion, the most comfortable position is crossing your legs and keeping the spine as straight as possible. Whichever position you take, you should be fully relaxed. If you are finding it difficult to maintain a certain posture, this is a sign that you are doing it incorrectly and that you should either shift to a more comfortable position or get the current one right.

Close your eyes and concentrate on your feelings and your awareness of your surroundings. Keep your eyes closed as you visualize and concentrate on the air passing through your skin, any sounds in your environment, and what the inner you is feeling at this particular time. Acknowledge everything that is happening around you, and ensure that your awareness is as robust as possible.

The main intent of Metta meditation is to encourage positivity and to ensure that you feel are in a position where you feel loved and can send out such love to the world. To achieve this, you need to find a mentality where you are feeling high levels of positivity. Begin by visualizing a person who loves you very much. This could be a family member, a lover, a close friend, or even your pet. Visualize that loved one standing before you, and sending their love to you. Not only is that person sending you good wishes for your safety and well-being, but they also offer assurance that you mean a lot to them and they will always treasure you. Feel the love as the person spreads positivity over your life, assuring you that you matter and that they treasure you.

Now, visualize three more loved ones, and picture them standing all around you. Just like the first person, these people are also speaking positivity, assuring you that they love you very much. At this point, more people have joined them, and they are all sending you warmth and love. You are overwhelmed by love, and your heart is bursting with joy. You can feel the love of all these people, and you are certain in your heart that, indeed, you are loved.

Now, shift your focus back to the initial person you visualized. At this time, he is quiet, and you are the one sending love. Begin by complimenting this person, making them aware of their strengths and all the wonderful qualities they possess. Wish the person happiness, joy, and all the positivity that life has to offer. Tell them how much you love them and how much you hope that all their desires may come to pass. At this time, you are a vessel overflowing with love and kindness, and you are extending such feelings to the rest of the world.

If you aren't sure what to do, focus on affirming the following three things:

"I am sorry."

"I forgive you."

"I love you."

Note that we are all human beings who are prone to error. You may have wronged someone without intending to and without awareness. When you tell someone these three simple lines, it is an illustration of the development of a clear conscience, which means you both can proceed with a healthy relationship.

Once you are done visualizing your friends, begin visualizing the acquaintances whom you don't have any feelings toward, and those whom you may have rubbed shoulders with in the wrong way. You may not know the impact of the three simple lines, but as soon as you say them and actually mean them, you become a new person. You will realize that you have let go of any anger you may have held toward these people, and you can approach them with a kinder demeanor. Ultimately, the positive energy that you are sending into the world will come back to you.

Day 2: The Body Scan Meditation

Once you've dealt with emotional issues on the first day, it's now time to deal with matters pertaining to the overall body and any concerns that may be affecting it. The body scan meditation involves laying on a flat surface and concentrating on how the physical body is feeling at that particular time. If you have pain in any part of the body, focus on that pain and try to deduce what caused them in the first place. As you carry out your body scan, you may be surprised to realize there are some issues in your body you may have been ignoring for a considerable amount of time.

The body scan should also concentrate on how you are feeling in terms of mental health and agility, and the resultant consequences that may arise from such feelings. For example, if you have any feelings of increased anxiety and stress, try to focus on them to determine the effects they have on your body.

One of the best ways of conducting a body scan meditation is taking your time and evaluating how you feel one organ after the other. You can choose to either start from the toes and work up to your head, or vice versa. Take it one step at a time and actually visualize what that part of the body is feeling. You may find there are some parts with increased tension, while others have sore muscles and inflammations. If you can correctly predict why such feelings and pains are there, you are on your way to developing strategies which can help in the prevention of similar pains in the future.

Some people may not be comfortable with the body scan meditation, particularly those who are already experiencing health concerns. For such people, focusing on how the body feels may end up affirming that they are sicker than they think, which results in increased anxiety and stress. If you know you are susceptible to these anxious feelings or that you may have some hypochondriac tendencies, you are likely better off avoiding this type of meditation.

On the other hand, if you want to be totally aware of everything that is going on around and within you, then this meditation will be perfect. Think of yourself as a musical instrument which is in constant need of being tuned. If you never come to terms with what is ailing you, then you never know what you should be dealing with in the long run.

Day 3: Breathing Exercises

Proper breathing is one of the tenets of meditation that contributes to its undoubted success. Whenever you are meditating, breathing is one of the factors you must take into consideration. Usually, the manner in which you are breathing dictates the position you may be in, both mentally and physically. For example, loud, erratic breaths are a representation of anxiety, fear, and stress, while slow, controlled breathing denotes peace and calm. As a beginner, you need to learn how to breathe efficiently while meditating. Since the main goal is to achieve a state of pure calm, how you breathe is very important.

The best breathing techniques include taking a deep breath in and letting it out carefully. Be slow when you are taking your breaths, and ensure you can actually feel the air filling your lungs and leaving them as you exhale. Concentrate on your chest moving up and down, and fill your lungs as much as possible, then empty them as best as you can in slow successions.

As you focus on the deep breaths, you will feel your body shift, and it becomes very calm and peaceful. It is only when you have mastered this breathing technique that you are in the process of achieving awareness and the insight of everything that affects us. The following steps will help you ensure that you master the breathing technique, preparing you to be a meditation pro.

The first step is choosing a location where you can lay flat on your back. This is the most appropriate position, although some enthusiasts may prefer to take up a yoga position.

The next step is to close your eyes and ensure that as little light as possible is in the room. Darkness is known to have a calming effect on the brain, while light keeps the mind active, which makes the meditation a little more difficult. If you are in an open location, wear sunglasses or the eye covers to block out as much light as possible.

Begin taking slow, deep breaths, and aim at attaining a particular number. For example, try to take ten deep breaths, and ensure that your focus is on breathing only — don't let your mind wander off. To build resilience and self-discipline, begin your count again whenever the mind strays and maintain your focus until you ultimately complete the desired cycle.

Practice these breathing exercises as much as you can, until you can do them without letting your mind wander.

Day 4: Self-Compassion Meditation

Self-compassion meditation is done one day after you have done the body scan meditation. This practice is inclined toward trying to focus on the issues identified in the body scan. The main point of self-compassion is to treat yourself well. You must aim at treating yourself the way you would treat a close friend who may be suffering. Therefore, not only does self-compassion include feelings of kindness and understanding, but it focuses on the notion that you can make something better when you put your mind to it.

To begin the meditation, lie on your back and focus on the areas you felt were not fully okay during the previous session. Accept that the human body is not perfect, and is susceptible to various conditions and ailments. Whenever you reach a point of acceptance, it is easier to deal with the underlying issue since you are no longer living in denial, and neither are you pitying yourself. It's simply nature, and you don't have to blame yourself for whatever it is that you are feeling at a particular time. Some people may blame themselves for ailments and focus on what they could have done to prevent it — a factor which clouds their mind to what they can do now to resolve it.

More importantly, fight off any feelings of self-loathing. You can never achieve self-compassion if you are always beating yourself up over things that you cannot change in the present moment. Note that when we talk concentrating on things that may not be working, we are not talking about obsessive thinking and the over-identification of shortcomings. Take it easy.

As you are laying down and focusing on these problematic areas, create a vision in the head where you are taking care of such parts by either rubbing, massaging, applying ointments. This vision should be limited to the exact place that is ailing you. Create your mental vision and feel the condition slowly going away. The mind has more power than you may know, and convincing it that you are getting better can actually manifest in how you are feeling. The more you affirm your healing, the more positively the body will respond. Ultimately, this hope and seeing your health improve will help you experience increased happiness, health, hope, and optimism.

However, you should not dwell on your discomfort or problematic areas for too long, since this may subconsciously make you feel even worse. Rather, focus on what you can do to improve the situation.

This self-compassion meditation should be done over ten to thirty minutes. If you find it hard to concentrate when it is too silent, or you know that you will likely fall asleep, put on some slow music.

Day 5: Gratitude Meditation

The gratitude meditation is aimed at concentrating on the positive things in your life. Embrace the goodness and ensure that you are focusing on you and not anyone else. Try to list at least ten things you are grateful for. The list can be as long as you wish — the more gratitude you have, the better your consciousness.

In this meditation, you should be fully conscious and at a place where you can comfortably write. List the items of gratitude one after the other, and really concentrate on each word you write. Gratitude meditations are very important and should be carried out after the self-compassion meditation, as they help in affirming that even though you may be having some issues with your body, there is still much more to be grateful about.

As you write down your list, it is important actually to own it by using the personal pronoun "I." Therefore, your list should look something like:

- I am beautiful

- I have a great job
- I have a great family
- I have big blue eyes, etc.

Ensure that whatever you write is not just for the sake of it, but that you believe every word. Don't write anything that you are doubtful about, since that will put your whole list in contention with your inner self. Take a moment to deeply appreciate each item you have written down. In the end, you will realize how valuable you are — this is the best way to deal with issues such as low self-esteem and self-worth.

This meditation can go as long as you want, as long as you maintain focus during the entire session. You can use your list for affirmations, which means it would be prudent to consistently repeat these things to yourself out loud, either when you are going to bed or as soon as you wake up. Not only do affirmations serve as a reminder, they also help in the molding of a more confident and seemingly limitless person.

Days 6 and 7: Resting and Silent Meditation

The brain is a muscle. Since meditations act as a brain gym, there will obviously be a need to rest. On day six, prepare the mind to rest by having a silent meditation. This meditation means that you do not have to focus on anything — you should stay silent and still and feel all the emotions and thoughts as they run through your mind. Unlike the other meditation practices, where you need to disregard these thoughts, the silent meditation involves acknowledging everything. You can think about the reasons as to why such thoughts are so deeply engrossed in you but, basically, just think normally.

On day seven, do not participate in any meditative practice. This is the day your brain should rest, and you should go about all the activities that you normally would without any instance of meditating.

Day 8: Guided Meditation

This is the first day of the second week, and it's a good idea to begin with a therapeutic meditation. Guided meditation is perfect, and all you need to do is either use audio with guidance or actually engage a meditation leader. Currently, there are very many places which offer yoga and meditation guidance, and you can attend one of them if you want a more personal touch.

Meditation leaders and audios provide step-by-step instructions which you must follow precisely. Most of these guided meditations are inclined towards leading you in a sort of trance, which is necessary for either relaxing you or helping you to visualize something. There is no time limitation in a guided meditation, and you can select audios or classes you feel will best suit you.

Day 9: Retrospective Meditation

The retrospective meditation encourages you to look back at a certain point in your life. You can analyze the events that happened during that day, week, month, or even year. For beginners, you should begin by focusing on the events of a specific day. Think about everything you did, whether you were productive or not, and the events that made you happy. You should also think about the things that were unsatisfactory and which may have made you sad or angry.

The major benefit of retrospective meditation is that you actually get an idea of why things happened the way they did, and how you can make any unsatisfactory events better in the future. For instance, if you had an altercation with your colleague, you can think about the events that led to it and some of the ways in which you could have prevented the occurrence. For example, if the colleague was angry at you because of some pending work that you had not completed, you already have your answer about how you can avoid a repeat of the same. By simply managing your time better and finishing your work by your deadline, you will have a better relationship with the person.

Thinking about the good occurrences will encourage you to keep up the practices that led to that so that more satisfaction can be experienced in the future. For example, if management was happy with a report you presented, think about how you prepared and the factors which contributed to such satisfaction. Once you get your answer, you will ultimately be better suited to employ the same techniques in your upcoming tasks.

Note that, since meditation is all about positivity, you should place more focus on what worked as opposed to any negative occurrences. However, the little focus on what did not work should be done with the main aim of forgiving oneself and others, and the identification of measures which can be undertaken in the future to prevent a repeat of the same.

This meditation is also not time conscious — you can carry on for as long as you maintain your focus.

Day 10: Visualization Meditation

Visualization meditation has already been discussed in depth, and it involves the creation of mental pictures about various matters of interest. For example, you may visualize a beautiful place that you would want to visit and create a mental picture of how such a place would look. Imagine yourself in this place, laughing and playing as you enjoy your surroundings. When it comes to visualization, your creativity is what is required, and there is no limit to how far you can go to. Examples of visualizations include:

- You are at a very lovely beach in a coastal town, and the water is blue and marvelous.
- You are with your loved ones in a serene place, and you are joyfully singing together.

- You have a very good job, and you are driving around in the car of your dreams.
- You have your own family, and you are in a park playing together.

Basically, visualize an image which gives you the highest level of satisfaction and fulfillment.

To begin the visualization meditation, ensure you are in a very comfortable position. You can either use the mat, chair, pillow, or cushion, and you can either carry it out while you are closing your eyes or when walking around in the open. You must only visualize happy places, people, or occurrences, and stretch your creativity as wide as possible. This meditation can go on as long as you wish, and you will realize an elevated sense of happiness and tranquility once you are done.

Day 11: Meditating About the People You Love

Meditating about the people you love not only gives you more insight into the contributions they have made in your life, but also helps you appreciate them more. By the time you begin meditating about these other people, you will have already meditated about yourself for as long and as much as you possibly can. With your newly-acquired personal love, you can now extend the same love to others.

There is no limit to the types of people that you could meditate about — they can range from your immediate family to your colleagues and friends. Choose a few family members and friends from your list and concentrate on them. Think about all the wonderful qualities they have and the positive ways in which they have impacted your life. Usually, the more you think about a person in a positive light, the more you recognize their worth and ultimately appreciate them.

When you make this type of meditation a habit, you will develop the ability to see the best in people, which will drastically improve your relationships with those around you. Further, you will be more appreciative of even the smallest things that people do for you and, in the process, become better positioned to develop long-lasting positive relationships with them. These relationships will undoubtedly help in the improvement of your mental and emotional status, which will make you live a life full of contentment.

Day 12: Manifestation Meditation

The manifestation meditation is amongst the types of meditations that will undoubtedly change your life for the better. Manifestation simply means striving to achieve your heart's desires, which can be in any area of your life. Everyone has their own goals and dreams, and these desires often change in accordance with factors such as age and priorities. For this meditation, concentrate on whatever it is you wish to accomplish at this particular time.

To manifest what you want in life, you must have a clear picture of what you want before you begin the meditation, and ensure it is something that can actually be achieved. This means that you have to distinguish between daydreaming and true potential dreams and aspirations.

Manifestation is a little different from the other types of meditation, and the fact that it is the last in this guide is because of the simple reason that it is more engaging and requires much more mental focus and agility. Manifestation is not easy, and you need to make sure that you are at a point where you can totally focus on something and disregard any other thoughts that may attempt to confuse you.

To effectively carry out the manifestation meditation, follow this procedure:

First, ensure that you established your subject of intent. This means you must have total clarity about whatever it is you wish to manifest. If it is finances, have a clear number of what you would regard to be stability. If it is healing, have clarity about the exact thing that is ailing you. Before you begin the manifestation, ensure that you have the will to proceed and the belief that whatever it is that you manifest shall eventually come to pass.

The second step is ensuring you are in a silent place, which is most conducive to meditation. You can select any place that appeals to you and ensures that you will be able to complete the practice without interference, since the manifestation focus should not shift.

At this point, you are ready to begin. Start by taking deep breaths in and out, and focus on your stomach moving up and down. Concentrate on the movements until you start feeling more clarity of thought. Focus on the subject of your intent and disregard any thoughts that may be attempting to convince you that what you are aiming for is impossible. Since the brain cannot be totally turned off, other thoughts are bound to cross your mind even as you are concentrating. Acknowledge them, take a deep breath, and, as you breathe out, let those thoughts go. This is the surest way of ensuring that you will be able to keep your focus solidified and clear.

One of the main things to keep in mind is that a manifestation is more than just focusing on a particular subject matter. You need to be so engrossed in the subject of your focus that you attach feelings and emotions to it. If it is a material thing, think about how it would make you feel if you owned it. Feel the joy and happiness that you believe you would if you were to have that object. When you attach these emotions, you make the manifestation more authentic and increase your desire to actually strive to get it.

Keep focusing and meditating until you are done. The session can either be timed or carried out until a time when you feel that you have meditated enough. Once you complete the meditation process, manifestation requires you to start behaving and acting like a person who has already received whatever they were manifesting. Manifestation works hand in hand with the law of attraction, where once you believe you will actually get whatever it is that you may be seeking, it will come your way.

Day 13 and 14

These are the end of week days, and you should follow the procedure outlined in days six and seven. Rest is very important, and these are the perfect days to relax your mind.

Best Time to Meditate

Meditation is not restrictive — you can practice it at any time of the day. People have different schedules and routines, which determines the times they consider to be most suitable for meditation. If you are not sure about the most appropriate time to meditate, the following are a few examples:

Early Mornings: Most people practice meditation early in the morning, within an hour or two of waking. One of the advantages of this is that practitioners have a greater chance of achieving a higher level of focus than if they had carried out the meditation at a different time. Typically, you are more refreshed and energized in the morning, since you will have just come out of deep sleep. Also, the mind will have not yet begun delving into the usual worries and concerns that tend to cause stress throughout the day, which means that it will be easier to stay in the present moment and focus. When you meditate in the morning, you set the tone and standard for the rest of the day, which means you will likely be more efficient and productive.

Right before you sleep: Some of us are just not morning people, and between waking up late and hurrying to work, there is not always time for meditation. Others are at their worst in the morning due to factors such as fatigue and insufficient sleep. If you fall into this category, you can always try to meditate right before you go to bed. The major benefit with this meditation is that it will actually help settle your mind and calm you down, which will increase your chances of having a more fulfilling sleep. Note that meditation does not have to take long — you can just set aside two minutes of your time for your practice.

During the day: All employees are subject to breaks in the course of carrying out their jobs. These breaks include time set aside for coffee and lunch. Most of the time, these breaks can last up to an hour, which gives you sufficient time to both enjoy your meal or snack and meditate. There is no restriction on where you should meditate, and you can even set aside a place in your office to do so.

Building an Altar

Setting up an altar is a practice that is typically done by

people who take meditation very seriously. Usually, the altar is not complex and is often made up of a table with a number of elements and tools placed upon it. Most people who go to the extent of building altars do so for spirituality and religious purposes, although there are others who do it simply for aesthetic value. If you wish to build an altar, here is a list of things you may consider including:

A Bell: A bell can serve multiple purposes, depending on the reason of your meditation. Some people like ringing it to illustrate the beginning of the session while others, such as the Wiccan witches, use it to invoke the spirits so that they can manifest during the practice.

Candles: Candles are a source of light, and are also associated with positive energy. When you use them, it is a sign that you are seeking the best out of the experience and that you are confident the results will be in your favor. Different colors of candles may also be used to affirm the focus of the meditation. For instance, since the color green is associated with abundance, you can burn a green candle when the subject of your meditation is wealth and abundance.

Flowers and Incense: These two are used for the simple reason of decoration, as well as providing good scents around the altar.

Chapter 4: Laws and Approaches to Meditation

Meditation is undoubtedly one of the most reliable tools that can be used in the management of some of our most critical emotions, as well as the secret to living a fulfilled life and connecting with your spirit. One of the ways through which you will gain a better understanding of the role meditation plays in the lives of practitioners is by considering its seven laws. These principles are behind the happy and fulfilled life that meditators experience and provide a better awareness of the methodology behind it. Each of these laws is deeply incorporated into meditation, and they are the main tenets that make up the practice.

1. Pure Potentiality

Human beings have great potential and are capable of achieving anything they put their kind to. As a person, you are like the waves of the oceans, which not only stretch far and wide but have the potential to destroy cities. This means that what you can achieve is much more than you can even comprehend. In as much as you are a conscious being, you may be blinded and unaware of your potential, which is why so many people don't even know what they want to achieve and end up living meaninglessly. Others seemingly have direction, although the truth is that they rarely live up to even half of their potential.

Meditation aims at connecting you to your spirit and opening your subconscious mind to guide you in the direction of your destiny. Whenever you visualize, you realize that all that you want and need is accessible, and you only need to act upon it to achieve your potential. Everything we wish for is reachable — all we need to do is act. When you meditate, you give yourself the chance to think about the multiple ways through which you can make some of your visualizations a reality, and there is a better chance that your mind will come up with ideas to propel you toward success. Act on those instincts, and you will undoubtedly realize the benefits.

2. Giving and Receiving

We have already learned that everything is made up of energy that is in continuous motion. Our actions determine the flow of energy, and you can either contribute to the abundance of positive or negative energy. But how we can ensure that we always contribute to the flow of positive energy?

Since everything is made of energy, if you hold on to something that can benefit others, you are restricting the flow. Consequently, whenever you help others through either actions or material form, you contribute to the circulation of positive energy. When it comes to meditation, this law of giving and receiving manifests through practitioners allowing thoughts to come and go with minimal resistance, and the ultimate allowance of senses such as sounds, texture, and color to be upon us with minimal restrictions.

This law is most prevalent when one is carrying out the manifestation meditation. Through your thoughts, you project to the universe the things that you would love to have, as well as what you wish to achieve. These thoughts provide you with an idea of how you can achieve whatever you are manifesting, which causes the thoughts to come back to you in the form of results.

3. Law of Karma

Everyone knows about karma, which is the belief that whatever you do will come back to you. Usually, karma is associated with bad occurrences. When you are aware of this law, you are bound to be more conscious and ensure that your interactions with other people bring them good, and not bad. Also, you will be more intent in your behaviors, as you know there is a price to pay for any choice you make.

Karma interacts with meditation through the simple process of cleansing the thoughts. As you know, meditation is inclined toward positivity, which means that you will ultimately be at harmony with yourself and the people around you. When you have pure and innocent thoughts about these people, you will be better able to treat them well and avoid any instances where you may hurt them, regardless of what they may have done to you. This helps keep negative karma at bay.

4. Law of the Least Effort

Meditation is a practice that requires little effort. Even though you may struggle a little as a beginner, especially with keeping your focus on single thoughts, you will realize that with time and practice, you can achieve this effortlessly. The act of meditation is based upon simple procedures such as breathing softly and focusing on the breath, as well as calming your mind and ensuring that other thoughts are mitigated.

If, in the process of meditation, you feel as if you are using too much energy and it is in some way cumbersome, it is a sign that you are doing it the wrong way. Also, if you feel extremely tired and worn out after completing the meditation, you are on the wrong track. Meditation is about stillness and least effort, and once you master it, you can employ a similar technique when you are carrying out other tasks.

5. Intention and Desire

Intention is considered to be a powerful force of nature that helps propel you to achieve anything you may want. When you mix intention with desire, you find a greater drive to accomplish whatever it is you are focused upon, and the result is more fulfillment in life.

When you begin practicing meditation, you will realize that your awareness of your own self increases significantly, giving you a clearer picture of the things you may want to achieve. Once you become conscious of these needs and wants, it is like sowing a seed, and the way you respond determines whether you will actually achieve the desired positive outcomes. Increased meditation will make your goal clearer, and it will be much easier to take the resultant steps to ensure you reach your goal.

6. Law of Detachment

The law of detachment stipulates that once you let the universe know about your desires, do not dwell on them — let them go. In their own time, they will manifest. This is similar to the law of attraction, which affirms that you must release any attachment you may have to the outcome, since that is the only way through which your desire will be fulfilled.

The meditation process helps you with the development of the spirit, which helps you let go of any expectations through the fostering of a calm demeanor, which is free of anxiety. Remember, you should not dwell on a single subject of focus for a long time, but you should meditate about different topics each day. You may not realize it, but shifting your focus allows you to let go of any expectations and attachment that you may have on the other subjects. Ultimately, you are bound to concentrate on your present accomplishments and successes, which will ensure you always live in the moment.

7. Dharma Law

The law of dharma encompasses the teachings that every person in the world has a specific purpose for which they were created. Therefore, you must cease living just for the sake of it, and you must develop the desire to live in accordance with the best of your potential. As religion teaches us, we all have special gifts we were meant to share with the world, and it is up to you to determine what your gift is. The biggest tragedy may be that the gifts are not always obvious, and some of us need to really look within ourselves to determine the gifts we possess.

The law of dharma relates to meditation in the sense that the latter helps us achieve a very high level of self-awareness. Therefore, when you begin looking deep within yourself, you may actually be able to unveil your unique gift, which will help you determine the ways in which you can share it with the world. If the situation you find yourself in is limiting, let it go and strive to reach the deep awareness that will propel you to greater heights.

Troubleshooting Some Problems While Meditating

By nature, meditation is supposed to make you calmer, peaceful, and more at ease with the various experiences you may be going through at a particular time. Naturally, taking deep breaths, visualizing things in a positive light, and repeating the different mantras are bound to make you more relaxed. With time, most people confess that they experience a total change, which means that they are no longer doing the negative things they used to do before they started meditating. For example, people who were susceptible to anger episodes confess that they no longer have such feelings, while people who may have previously hated others confess that meditation helped them to be more accepting of different individualities. But what if you are experiencing the opposite?

Let us assume that the meditation process is seemingly not working for you. You have already meditated about yourself and your colleagues, but your feelings have not changed in the least. Where you had trouble with some of your colleagues, the relationship is increasingly strained. The more you meditate about your condition and health, the worse you feel. What are you supposed to do in such a situation?

The first thing you need to understand is that you are not alone. There are plenty of other meditators with the same challenge, and you should not be too hard on yourself. Meditation is not a quick fix, which means that at the end of the day, you will still have to react to the various issues you may be facing. However, try to be as positive as you can and attempt to see the good in everything. With time, the positive attitude will grow on you, and you will find it much easier to deal with any difficult situation. For now, just focus on what is working.

Sometimes, you may be carried away as you are meditating, and you may find that your focus is on something totally disruptive. For example, you may be meditating about your friends when a thought crosses your mind about an altercation you may have had with them, which then ruins your meditation process as you start wondering if the attention you are giving them is really worth it. Whenever this happens, it is imperative that you learn how to embrace those thoughts and feelings, acknowledge them, and work on letting them go before you begin meditating once again. The more you own your feelings and emotions, the better you can shift your awareness and deal with them.

As you follow meditation guides, you may find that you are having a hard time remembering the instructions. Obviously, you cannot keep opening your eyes to read the instructions, as that will mess with your focus and shift your attention to something else. One of the best ways of dealing with this problem is owning the meditation by not only reading the instructions, but rephrasing it in a manner which will make it easier to remember. You can write the steps in a simplified manner and study them so that when you begin the meditation process, you already know what to do without referring back to the texts.

Other times, you may be in the midst of extreme emotions when you want to meditate. For example, someone may have deeply angered you just before you began meditating, and you may realize that you still have lingering anger even as you are proceeding with your practice. In such a situation, the best thing you can do is strive to determine the effect the emotion has on you at a particular time. For example, you may focus on the parts of your body where you are feeling the tension and actual pain as a result of inflammation. Notice how the anger is having an effect on your breathing and heart rate, then determine if the person or occurrence that upset you is really worth it. Do not focus on any other topic until you've dealt with the anger. Think about some of the things that you would have done to prevent the situation from becoming aggravated and promise yourself that, in the future, you will choose this better option. Attempt to identify the point at which you start relaxing, and the thoughts that are contributing to this relaxation. These are the thoughts that you should invoke the next time you are angry. Once you've fully calmed down, you can begin the meditation you intended.

Fear and anxiety are other emotions that can influence how you conduct your meditation. It is human nature to be afraid and get anxious sometimes, and meditation is one of the ways through which you can overcome this. Just like how you dealt with anger, it is important to begin by trying to identify the parts of the body with tension, as well as the physical consequences that you realize from fear and anxiety. Also, focus on the effect the fear has on your breathing and heartbeat. Most importantly, you must determine the thoughts and feelings that are accompanying the fear. Once done, attempt to analyze the onset of the fear, and the factors which may have contributed to it. If it is something from your childhood or youth that you may not have dealt with efficiently, start thinking of ways to make the situation better. This will mark the beginning of your healing, and you will be better positioned to achieve uninterrupted meditation in the future. Wait until the fear and anxiety has worn off, and your breath and heartbeat are regulated, to begin meditating on your preferred topic.

Finally, you may be experiencing grief and sadness, battling with pain, or feeling extremely low. One upside of grief and sadness is that people find these emotions much easier to express compared to other extreme feelings such as anger. This ease of expression is particularly prevalent among women — it is rather sad to see men struggling with their problems in silence, if they were taught that showing emotion is showing weakness. Note that you must express the emotion you experience to more effectively deal with it.

Before you begin meditating on the subject of your choice, ensure the sadness has space to express itself, and come to terms with what you are feeling. Do not try to convince yourself that you are not feeling the emotion, since that is just deception — it will result in you not dealing with the problem from the root. Pay close attention to the thoughts that are contributing to these feelings and acknowledge them. If you can, amplify the emotion and cry if you have to. You will realize that whenever you cry, you end up feeling much better, which is what you want. When you are done, visualize the particular things you can do to prevent a similar occurrence, and do away with any self-defeating thoughts. When your mood has improved, begin the meditation.

Key Takeaways

There are a number of key takeaways that can be deduced from this topic of meditation. Some of the major ones include:

➢ Meditation is the window to which we gain access to our subconscious minds and increase our overall level of awareness. When we meditate, it is likened to the mirroring of the soul, and we are able to gain deeper insights we didn't even know were possible.

➢ Meditation is the absolute opposite of emotions. When we meditate, we tend to acknowledge things as they are and, in the process, become more trusting and accepting of the different situations we face. This is very different from emotions, which are the root of chaos and drama in our lives. Whenever we involve emotions in something, be it positive or negative, we are more likely to overthink, and in the process, we can make situations that were not even very serious worse. For example, let's assume that we're dealing with a romantic situation. If that relationship ends, meditation will be able to calm us down and even enlighten us more to the different situations that may have resulted in the collapse of the relationship. Further, we are better able to critically assess the situation and look at it from a different point of view, which enables us to fully accept the situation as it is. This is very different from emotions, which often result in feelings such as betrayal and increased hurt. In the end, you may end up being very bitter.

- There's no way to avoid all the negativity that is likely to come your way. For instance, pain and suffering are just part of human life, and at some point or the other, you are bound to experience one or both. Through meditation, there is a higher likelihood that you will be able to accept the situation and work to improve it. Therefore, meditation is one of the best escapes from negative situations.

- Through meditation, many ailments can be mitigated. Mental disorders, such as depression and anxiety, can be better managed through meditation. The fact that the practice calms you down and brings you to terms with your different conditions means you will have an easier time coping and ultimately prevent such disorders from impacting you.

- There are multiple types of meditations, and you should practice the one that most appeals to you, as well as which relates to your situation. For example, if you wish to manifest something, choose the manifestation meditation. Likewise, you can conduct the awareness meditation when you want to learn about yourself and what you can offer to the world.

- There are a number of things that meditation is confused with, and they include praying, daydreaming, affirmations, and normal thinking. All these are very different from meditation, which solely involves the connection with the deeper spirits and focus on an individual and very specific subject matter.

- There are very many benefits of meditation, which include:
  - Better emotional health
  - Increased self-awareness
  - Improved attention
  - Control of anxiety
  - Improved memory
  - Generation of kindness
  - Fighting of addictions
  - Improved sleep

- Meditation is very simple — the only things you require to begin are a personal space, timer, and the actual will to practice.

- You must keep in mind the following before you embark on meditation:
  - The mind can never go blank — there will always be some form of activity during

meditation.

- There is no one posture necessitated in meditation, and you should adopt the posture which makes you feel the most comfortable.

- There are many sources for meditation practices, ranging from books and individual tutors to online sources.

- The practice has been around for multiple years.

- You can never be too busy for meditation, since the practice can be successfully undertaken for as little as two minutes.

- Meditation is a form of exercise for the brain. The more you meditate, the healthier the brain becomes.

- Just like with any other exercise, ensure you take breaks from time to time. Use these breaks to reflect on the different areas you have covered in meditation and how they have impacted your life to date.

References

Balázs, J., Miklósi, M., Keresztény, Á., Hoven, C. W., Carli, V., Wasserman, C., ... & Cotter, P. (2013). Adolescent subthreshold-depression and anxiety: Psychopathology, functional impairment and increased suicide risk. *Journal of child psychology and psychiatry*, *54*(6), 670-677.

Downing, C. J. (1986). affirmations: steps to counter negative, self-fulfilling prophecies. *Elementary School Guidance & Counseling*, *20*(3), 174-179.

Spielberger, C. D. (Ed.). (2013). Anxiety: Current trends in theory and research. Elsevier.

MeditationTeam. (2019). Where Does Meditation Come From? Meditation History & Origins. Retrieved 31 July 2019, from https://mindworks.org/blog/history-origins-of-meditation/

Printed in Great Britain
by Amazon